50 Korean Side Recipes for Home

By: Kelly Johnson

Table of Contents

- Kimchi (Napa cabbage or radish)
- Pickled cucumbers (Oi-sobagi)
- Stir-fried spinach (Sigeumchi namul)
- Seasoned bean sprouts (Kongnamul muchim)
- Stir-fried fish cakes (Eomuk bokkeum)
- Stir-fried shredded potatoes (Gamjajeon)
- Spicy cucumber salad (Oi-muchim)
- Seasoned dried shredded squid (Ojingeochae-muchim)
- Stir-fried tofu with soy sauce (Dubu jorim)
- Stir-fried zucchini (Hobak bokkeum)
- Seasoned dried anchovies (Myeolchi bokkeum)
- Braised lotus root (Yeonkeun jorim)
- Sweet and sour radish salad (Musengchae)
- Pan-fried tofu with spicy sauce (Dubu buchim)
- Seasoned perilla leaves (Kkaennip muchim)
- Pan-fried fish cakes (Eomuk jeon)
- Braised potatoes (Gamja jorim)
- Seasoned dried seaweed (Miyeok muchim)
- Stir-fried cabbage (Baechu bokkeum)
- Seasoned spinach (Sigeumchi-muchim)
- Stir-fried mushrooms (Beoseot bokkeum)
- Braised dried anchovies (Myeolchi jorim)
- Seasoned radish salad (Musaengchae)
- Pan-fried pancakes with vegetables (Pajeon)
- Stir-fried shredded squid (Ojingeo bokkeum)
- Braised burdock roots (Ueong jorim)
- Seasoned mung bean sprouts (Sukju namul)
- Steamed egg custard (Gyeran jjim)
- Stir-fried soybean sprouts (Kongnamul bokkeum)
- Pan-fried tofu with soy sauce (Dubu ganjangjorim)
- Spicy stir-fried squid (Ojingeo bokkeum)
- Braised lotus root with soy sauce (Yeonkeun jangajji)
- Seasoned perilla seeds (Deulkkae jangajji)
- Braised dried radish greens (Mu saengchae jorim)
- Stir-fried shredded dried squid (Ojingeochae bokkeum)

- Spicy stir-fried pork belly (Dwaeji bulgogi)
- Stir-fried spicy octopus (Nakji bokkeum)
- Seasoned dried pollack (Bugeo muchim)
- Pan-fried tofu with spicy sauce (Dubu buchim-yangnyeom)
- Stir-fried dried anchovies with peanuts (Kongari-myeolchi bokkeum)
- Spicy cucumber salad with vinegar (Oi-muchim)
- Stir-fried fish cake with vegetables (Eomuk bokkeum)
- Stir-fried dried anchovies with peanuts (Kongari-myeolchi bokkeum)
- Seasoned burdock roots (Ueong muchim)
- Pan-fried fish cakes with egg batter (Eomuk jeon)
- Stir-fried shredded dried squid with vegetables (Ojingeochae bokkeum)
- Braised dried anchovies with kelp (Myeolchi-muchim)
- Stir-fried dried shredded squid with vegetables (Ojingeo chae bokkeum)
- Spicy stir-fried squid with vegetables (Ojingeo bokkeum)
- Stir-fried dried anchovies with peanuts (Kongari-myeolchi bokkeum)

Kimchi (Napa cabbage or radish)

Ingredients:

- 1 large Napa cabbage
- 1/2 cup coarse sea salt
- 4 cups water
- 1 daikon radish, julienned (optional)
- 4-5 green onions, cut into 1-inch pieces
- 1/4 cup Korean red pepper flakes (gochugaru)
- 1/4 cup fish sauce (or soy sauce for vegan version)
- 1/4 cup finely minced garlic
- 1 tablespoon finely minced ginger
- 1 tablespoon sugar
- 1 teaspoon salted shrimp paste (saeujeot) or anchovy sauce (optional, omit for vegan version)

Instructions:

1. Cut the Napa cabbage lengthwise into quarters, then cut each quarter in half crosswise. Rinse the cabbage quarters under cold water and shake off excess water.
2. In a large bowl, dissolve the coarse sea salt in water to create a brine. Submerge the cabbage quarters in the brine, making sure they are fully covered. Let them soak for 2-3 hours, flipping them occasionally.
3. While the cabbage is soaking, prepare the seasoning paste. In a separate bowl, combine the Korean red pepper flakes, fish sauce (or soy sauce), minced garlic, minced ginger, sugar, and salted shrimp paste or anchovy sauce (if using). Mix well to form a thick paste.
4. After soaking, rinse the cabbage quarters thoroughly under cold water to remove excess salt. Gently squeeze out any excess water.
5. Spread a layer of the seasoning paste between each layer of cabbage leaves, making sure to coat each leaf evenly. Optionally, you can also add julienned daikon radish and green onion pieces between the layers.
6. Tightly roll up each cabbage quarter and place them in a clean, airtight container, pressing down firmly to remove any air pockets.
7. Seal the container and let it ferment at room temperature for 1-2 days to kick-start the fermentation process.

8. After 1-2 days, transfer the kimchi to the refrigerator and let it continue to ferment for at least 1 week before consuming. The longer it ferments, the tangier and more flavorful it will become.
9. Serve the kimchi as a side dish with rice, noodles, or any Korean meal. It can also be used as an ingredient in various dishes like kimchi fried rice, kimchi stew, or kimchi pancakes.

Enjoy the homemade Napa cabbage kimchi with its tangy, spicy, and umami flavors! Adjust the seasoning according to your taste preferences, and feel free to experiment with different vegetables and spices to create your own variations of kimchi.

Pickled cucumbers (Oi-sobagi)

Ingredients:

- 4-6 small Korean cucumbers (or 2-3 English cucumbers)
- 1/4 cup coarse sea salt
- 1 cup water
- 1/2 cup rice vinegar
- 2 tablespoons sugar
- 2 cloves garlic, minced
- 1 tablespoon grated ginger
- 2 green onions, thinly sliced
- 1/4 cup Korean red pepper flakes (gochugaru)
- 1 tablespoon sesame seeds
- 1 tablespoon sesame oil

Instructions:

1. Wash the cucumbers thoroughly under cold water. If using Korean cucumbers, slice off the stem ends. If using English cucumbers, peel strips of skin lengthwise to create a striped pattern. Slice each cucumber lengthwise into quarters, leaving about 1/2 inch intact at the bottom to hold the quarters together.
2. Dissolve the coarse sea salt in water to create a brine. Submerge the cucumber quarters in the brine, making sure they are fully covered. Let them soak for about 30 minutes to soften.
3. In a mixing bowl, combine rice vinegar, sugar, minced garlic, grated ginger, sliced green onions, Korean red pepper flakes, sesame seeds, and sesame oil. Mix well to create the stuffing mixture.
4. After 30 minutes, remove the cucumber quarters from the brine and drain excess water.
5. Stuff the cucumber quarters with the prepared stuffing mixture, making sure to distribute it evenly between the slices.
6. Place the stuffed cucumbers in a clean, airtight container or glass jar, stacking them tightly to keep them in place.
7. Seal the container and let it sit at room temperature for about 24 hours to allow the flavors to develop.

8. After 24 hours, transfer the container to the refrigerator and let the cucumbers continue to pickle for at least 2-3 days before consuming.
9. Serve the oi-sobagi chilled as a refreshing and flavorful side dish. It pairs well with rice, grilled meats, and other Korean dishes.

Enjoy the tangy and spicy flavors of homemade oi-sobagi! Adjust the seasoning according to your taste preferences, and feel free to experiment with different ingredients to create your own variations.

Stir-fried spinach (Sigeumchi namul)

Ingredients:

- 1 pound fresh spinach
- 1 tablespoon sesame oil
- 2 cloves garlic, minced
- 1 tablespoon soy sauce
- 1 teaspoon sesame seeds
- Salt, to taste
- Optional: sliced green onions for garnish

Instructions:

1. Rinse the spinach thoroughly under cold water to remove any dirt or grit. Trim off any tough stems.
2. Bring a large pot of water to a boil. Blanch the spinach in the boiling water for about 1-2 minutes, or until wilted but still vibrant green.
3. Drain the spinach and rinse it under cold water to stop the cooking process. Squeeze out excess water from the spinach using your hands.
4. Heat sesame oil in a large skillet or wok over medium heat. Add minced garlic and stir-fry for about 30 seconds, or until fragrant.
5. Add the blanched spinach to the skillet and stir-fry for 2-3 minutes, or until heated through.
6. Drizzle soy sauce over the spinach and continue to stir-fry for another 1-2 minutes, allowing the flavors to meld together.
7. Remove the skillet from the heat and sprinkle sesame seeds over the spinach. Toss to combine.
8. Taste the spinach and adjust the seasoning with salt, if needed.
9. Transfer the stir-fried spinach to a serving dish and garnish with sliced green onions, if desired.
10. Serve the sigeumchi namul as a side dish with rice and other Korean dishes.

Enjoy the delicious and nutritious flavors of homemade sigeumchi namul! Feel free to adjust the seasonings and add other ingredients like chopped onions or red pepper flakes to customize the dish to your taste.

Seasoned bean sprouts (Kongnamul muchim)

Ingredients:

- 1 pound bean sprouts
- 2 cloves garlic, minced
- 2 green onions, thinly sliced
- 1 tablespoon soy sauce
- 1 tablespoon sesame oil
- 1 tablespoon sesame seeds
- 1 teaspoon sugar
- 1 teaspoon vinegar (rice vinegar or apple cider vinegar)
- Salt, to taste
- Optional: red pepper flakes for heat, sliced carrots or bell peppers for added crunch

Instructions:

1. Rinse the bean sprouts thoroughly under cold water and drain well.
2. Bring a pot of water to a boil. Add the bean sprouts to the boiling water and blanch them for about 1-2 minutes, or until they are tender-crisp. Do not overcook them.
3. Drain the bean sprouts and rinse them under cold water to stop the cooking process. Drain well and pat them dry with paper towels.
4. In a large mixing bowl, combine the blanched bean sprouts with minced garlic, thinly sliced green onions, soy sauce, sesame oil, sesame seeds, sugar, vinegar, and salt. Mix well to coat the bean sprouts evenly with the seasoning.
5. Taste the seasoned bean sprouts and adjust the seasoning according to your taste preferences. Add more salt, soy sauce, sugar, or vinegar as needed.
6. If desired, add a pinch of red pepper flakes for a spicy kick, or toss in some sliced carrots or bell peppers for added crunch and color.
7. Transfer the seasoned bean sprouts to a serving dish and garnish with additional sesame seeds and green onions, if desired.
8. Serve the kongnamul muchim as a side dish with rice and other Korean dishes. It's also delicious as a topping for bibimbap or as a filling for Korean-style lettuce wraps.

Enjoy the refreshing and flavorful taste of homemade kongnamul muchim! This versatile side dish is perfect for adding a burst of flavor and texture to any meal. Adjust the seasonings and add your favorite vegetables to make it your own.

Stir-fried fish cakes (Eomuk bokkeum)

Ingredients:

- 200g fish cakes (eomuk), thinly sliced
- 1 tablespoon vegetable oil
- 2 cloves garlic, minced
- 1 small onion, thinly sliced
- 1 small carrot, julienned
- 2 green onions, sliced
- 2 tablespoons soy sauce
- 1 tablespoon sugar
- 1 tablespoon sesame oil
- Sesame seeds, for garnish
- Optional: sliced red or green chili peppers for heat

Instructions:

1. Heat the vegetable oil in a large skillet or wok over medium-high heat.
2. Add the minced garlic and stir-fry for about 30 seconds, until fragrant.
3. Add the thinly sliced fish cakes to the skillet and stir-fry for 2-3 minutes, until they start to brown slightly.
4. Add the sliced onion and julienned carrot to the skillet and continue to stir-fry for another 2-3 minutes, until the vegetables are tender-crisp.
5. In a small bowl, mix together the soy sauce and sugar until the sugar is dissolved.
6. Pour the soy sauce mixture over the stir-fried fish cakes and vegetables. Stir well to coat everything evenly.
7. Cook for another 1-2 minutes, until the sauce has thickened slightly and coats the fish cakes and vegetables.
8. Remove the skillet from the heat and drizzle sesame oil over the top. Toss everything together to combine.
9. Transfer the stir-fried fish cakes to a serving dish and garnish with sliced green onions and sesame seeds.
10. Optionally, sprinkle sliced red or green chili peppers over the top for added heat.
11. Serve the eomuk bokkeum as a side dish with rice and other Korean dishes.

Enjoy the savory and slightly sweet flavor of homemade stir-fried fish cakes! Adjust the seasoning according to your taste preferences, and feel free to add other vegetables like bell peppers or mushrooms for extra flavor and texture.

Stir-fried shredded potatoes (Gamjajeon)

Ingredients:

- 2 large potatoes
- 2 tablespoons vegetable oil
- 2 cloves garlic, minced
- 1 small onion, thinly sliced
- Salt, to taste
- Black pepper, to taste
- Optional: chopped green onions for garnish

Instructions:

1. Peel the potatoes and rinse them under cold water. Use a grater or a mandoline slicer to shred the potatoes into thin strips. Place the shredded potatoes in a bowl of cold water to prevent them from browning.
2. Heat the vegetable oil in a large skillet or frying pan over medium heat.
3. Drain the shredded potatoes and pat them dry with paper towels to remove excess moisture.
4. Add the minced garlic to the hot oil and stir-fry for about 30 seconds, until fragrant.
5. Add the sliced onion to the skillet and stir-fry for 1-2 minutes, until softened.
6. Increase the heat to medium-high and add the shredded potatoes to the skillet. Spread them out evenly in the pan.
7. Let the potatoes cook undisturbed for 3-4 minutes, allowing them to brown on the bottom. Use a spatula to flip the potatoes over and cook for another 3-4 minutes on the other side, until golden brown and crispy.
8. Season the stir-fried potatoes with salt and black pepper, to taste. Toss everything together to combine.
9. Transfer the gamjajeon to a serving dish and garnish with chopped green onions, if desired.
10. Serve the stir-fried shredded potatoes hot as a side dish with rice and other Korean dishes.

Enjoy the crispy and flavorful taste of homemade gamjajeon! Feel free to adjust the seasoning and add other ingredients like red pepper flakes or chopped bell peppers for extra flavor.

Spicy cucumber salad (Oi-muchim)

Ingredients:

- 2-3 small cucumbers or 1 English cucumber
- 1 teaspoon salt
- 2 cloves garlic, minced
- 1 tablespoon Korean red pepper flakes (gochugaru)
- 1 tablespoon rice vinegar or apple cider vinegar
- 1 tablespoon soy sauce
- 1 teaspoon sugar
- 1 teaspoon sesame oil
- 1 teaspoon toasted sesame seeds
- Optional: sliced green onions or cilantro for garnish

Instructions:

1. Rinse the cucumbers under cold water and pat them dry with a clean kitchen towel. If using small cucumbers, cut them into thin slices. If using an English cucumber, you can cut it into thin half-moon slices or julienne strips.
2. Place the cucumber slices in a colander or a large bowl and sprinkle them with salt. Toss to coat evenly and let them sit for about 10-15 minutes to draw out excess moisture.
3. Meanwhile, prepare the seasoning mixture. In a small bowl, combine minced garlic, Korean red pepper flakes, rice vinegar, soy sauce, sugar, sesame oil, and toasted sesame seeds. Mix well to dissolve the sugar and combine the ingredients.
4. After the cucumbers have rested, gently squeeze them to remove excess water and transfer them to a clean bowl.
5. Pour the prepared seasoning mixture over the cucumbers and toss to coat evenly. Use your hands to massage the seasoning into the cucumbers for better flavor absorption.
6. Let the cucumber salad marinate in the refrigerator for at least 30 minutes to allow the flavors to meld together.
7. Before serving, garnish the spicy cucumber salad with sliced green onions or cilantro, if desired.

8. Serve the Oi-muchim as a side dish with rice, grilled meats, or other Korean dishes.

Enjoy the refreshing crunch and spicy kick of homemade Oi-muchim! Adjust the seasoning according to your taste preferences, and feel free to add more or less red pepper flakes for your desired level of heat.

Seasoned dried shredded squid (Ojingeochae-muchim)

Ingredients:

- 100g dried shredded squid
- 2 tablespoons soy sauce
- 1 tablespoon gochugaru (Korean red pepper flakes)
- 1 tablespoon sesame oil
- 1 tablespoon honey or sugar
- 1 tablespoon rice vinegar or apple cider vinegar
- 1 clove garlic, minced
- 1 teaspoon sesame seeds
- Optional: sliced green onions for garnish

Instructions:

1. Rinse the dried shredded squid under cold water to remove any dust or debris. Soak the squid in warm water for about 15-20 minutes to soften it. Drain well and pat dry with paper towels.
2. In a small bowl, mix together the soy sauce, gochugaru, sesame oil, honey or sugar, rice vinegar, minced garlic, and sesame seeds to make the seasoning sauce.
3. Place the softened dried shredded squid in a mixing bowl and pour the seasoning sauce over it. Toss well to coat the squid evenly with the sauce.
4. Let the seasoned squid marinate in the refrigerator for at least 1 hour, or overnight for best flavor.
5. Before serving, garnish the Ojingeochae-muchim with sliced green onions, if desired.
6. Serve the seasoned dried shredded squid as a side dish with rice or as a snack.

Enjoy the savory and slightly spicy flavor of homemade Ojingeochae-muchim! Adjust the seasoning according to your taste preferences, and feel free to add more or less gochugaru for your desired level of spiciness.

Stir-fried tofu with soy sauce (Dubu jorim)

Ingredients:

- 1 block (14-16 oz) firm tofu
- 2 tablespoons soy sauce
- 1 tablespoon sesame oil
- 1 tablespoon brown sugar
- 1 tablespoon rice vinegar
- 2 cloves garlic, minced
- 1 teaspoon sesame seeds
- 1 green onion, thinly sliced (optional)
- 1 tablespoon vegetable oil, for frying

Instructions:

1. Start by preparing the tofu. Remove it from the package and drain any excess water. Then, wrap the tofu block in a clean kitchen towel and place a heavy object on top to press out more moisture. Let it sit for about 15-20 minutes.
2. While the tofu is pressing, prepare the sauce. In a small bowl, combine the soy sauce, sesame oil, brown sugar, rice vinegar, minced garlic, and sesame seeds. Mix well until the sugar is dissolved and all the ingredients are combined.
3. Once the tofu is pressed, cut it into bite-sized cubes or rectangular pieces, depending on your preference.
4. Heat the vegetable oil in a large skillet or frying pan over medium-high heat. Once the oil is hot, add the tofu pieces in a single layer, making sure not to overcrowd the pan. Fry the tofu for 3-4 minutes on each side, or until golden brown and crispy.
5. Once the tofu is cooked, reduce the heat to medium and pour the sauce over the tofu in the pan. Toss gently to coat the tofu evenly with the sauce.
6. Continue to cook for another 2-3 minutes, allowing the sauce to thicken slightly and coat the tofu.
7. Remove the pan from the heat and transfer the stir-fried tofu to a serving dish.
8. Garnish with sliced green onions, if desired, and serve hot as a side dish or protein addition to a meal.

Enjoy the savory and delicious flavor of homemade Dubu jorim! Adjust the seasoning according to your taste preferences, and feel free to add more or less soy sauce, sugar, or garlic to suit your taste.

Stir-fried zucchini (Hobak bokkeum)

Ingredients:

- 2 medium zucchinis
- 2 cloves garlic, minced
- 1 tablespoon soy sauce
- 1 tablespoon sesame oil
- 1 teaspoon sugar
- 1 teaspoon sesame seeds
- 1 tablespoon vegetable oil, for stir-frying
- Salt and pepper, to taste
- Optional: sliced green onions for garnish

Instructions:

1. Wash the zucchinis thoroughly under cold water. Trim off both ends and slice them into thin rounds or half-moons, depending on your preference.
2. Heat vegetable oil in a large skillet or wok over medium-high heat.
3. Add minced garlic to the skillet and stir-fry for about 30 seconds, until fragrant.
4. Add the sliced zucchinis to the skillet and stir-fry for 3-4 minutes, or until they start to soften but are still slightly crisp.
5. In a small bowl, mix together soy sauce, sesame oil, sugar, and sesame seeds to make the sauce.
6. Pour the sauce over the stir-fried zucchinis and toss well to coat evenly.
7. Continue to stir-fry for another 1-2 minutes, until the zucchinis are cooked through and the sauce has thickened slightly.
8. Season with salt and pepper, to taste, and toss again to combine.
9. Remove the skillet from the heat and transfer the stir-fried zucchinis to a serving dish.
10. Garnish with sliced green onions, if desired, and serve hot as a side dish with rice or other Korean dishes.

Enjoy the savory and flavorful taste of homemade Hobak bokkeum! Adjust the seasoning according to your taste preferences, and feel free to add other vegetables like bell peppers or carrots for extra flavor and color.

Seasoned dried anchovies (Myeolchi bokkeum)

Ingredients:

- 1 cup dried anchovies (myeolchi), heads and guts removed
- 2 tablespoons soy sauce
- 1 tablespoon honey or sugar
- 1 tablespoon gochujang (Korean red pepper paste)
- 1 tablespoon sesame oil
- 1 tablespoon toasted sesame seeds
- 2 cloves garlic, minced
- 1 teaspoon rice vinegar or apple cider vinegar
- 1 teaspoon vegetable oil, for frying

Instructions:

1. Rinse the dried anchovies under cold water to remove any impurities. Pat them dry with paper towels.
2. Heat vegetable oil in a large skillet or frying pan over medium heat. Once the oil is hot, add the dried anchovies and stir-fry for 1-2 minutes, until they are slightly crispy. Remove them from the pan and set aside.
3. In a small bowl, mix together soy sauce, honey or sugar, gochujang, sesame oil, minced garlic, and rice vinegar to make the seasoning sauce.
4. Heat the same skillet or frying pan over medium heat. Add the seasoning sauce to the pan and bring it to a simmer.
5. Once the sauce is simmering, add the stir-fried dried anchovies back to the pan. Toss them in the sauce until they are evenly coated.
6. Cook for another 2-3 minutes, stirring occasionally, until the sauce has thickened slightly and the anchovies are well-coated.
7. Sprinkle toasted sesame seeds over the anchovies and toss to combine.
8. Remove the pan from the heat and transfer the seasoned dried anchovies to a serving dish.
9. Serve hot or at room temperature as a side dish or snack.

Enjoy the savory, sweet, and slightly spicy flavor of homemade Myeolchi bokkeum! Adjust the seasoning according to your taste preferences, and feel free to add more or less gochujang for your desired level of spiciness.

Braised lotus root (Yeonkeun jorim)

Ingredients:

- 2 lotus roots, peeled and thinly sliced
- 2 cups water
- 2 tablespoons soy sauce
- 1 tablespoon sugar
- 1 tablespoon sesame oil
- 1 tablespoon rice vinegar or apple cider vinegar
- 2 cloves garlic, minced
- 1 teaspoon sesame seeds
- Optional: sliced green onions for garnish

Instructions:

1. Peel the lotus roots and slice them thinly crosswise into rounds. Rinse the slices under cold water to remove any dirt or debris.
2. In a large pot, combine water, soy sauce, sugar, sesame oil, rice vinegar, and minced garlic. Bring the mixture to a boil over medium-high heat.
3. Once the liquid is boiling, add the sliced lotus roots to the pot. Reduce the heat to medium-low and simmer, covered, for about 15-20 minutes, or until the lotus roots are tender.
4. Once the lotus roots are tender, remove the lid and continue to simmer for another 5-10 minutes, or until the liquid has reduced and thickened slightly.
5. Taste the braised lotus roots and adjust the seasoning with more soy sauce or sugar, if needed.
6. Sprinkle sesame seeds over the braised lotus roots and toss to coat evenly.
7. Transfer the braised lotus roots to a serving dish and garnish with sliced green onions, if desired.
8. Serve hot or at room temperature as a side dish with rice and other Korean dishes.

Enjoy the savory and tender flavor of homemade Yeonkeun jorim! Adjust the seasoning according to your taste preferences, and feel free to add other ingredients like ginger or chili peppers for extra flavor.

Sweet and sour radish salad (Musengchae)

Ingredients:

- 1 large Korean radish (mu) or daikon radish
- 2 tablespoons rice vinegar or apple cider vinegar
- 2 tablespoons sugar
- 1 teaspoon salt
- 1 teaspoon sesame oil
- 1 teaspoon sesame seeds
- Optional: sliced green onions or red chili flakes for garnish

Instructions:

1. Peel the radish and rinse it under cold water. Use a mandoline slicer or a sharp knife to julienne the radish into thin strips. Place the julienned radish in a large mixing bowl.
2. In a small bowl, mix together rice vinegar, sugar, and salt until the sugar and salt are dissolved.
3. Pour the vinegar mixture over the julienned radish in the mixing bowl. Toss well to coat the radish evenly with the dressing.
4. Let the radish marinate in the vinegar mixture for about 30 minutes to allow the flavors to meld together.
5. After marinating, drain any excess liquid from the radish. Add sesame oil and sesame seeds to the radish and toss to combine.
6. Taste the salad and adjust the seasoning with more salt or sugar, if needed.
7. Transfer the sweet and sour radish salad to a serving dish and garnish with sliced green onions or red chili flakes, if desired.
8. Serve chilled as a refreshing side dish with rice and other Korean dishes.

Enjoy the tangy and crunchy flavor of homemade Musengchae! Adjust the seasoning according to your taste preferences, and feel free to add other ingredients like garlic or ginger for extra flavor.

Pan-fried tofu with spicy sauce (Dubu buchim)

Ingredients:

- 1 block (14-16 oz) firm tofu
- 2 tablespoons soy sauce
- 1 tablespoon gochujang (Korean red pepper paste)
- 1 tablespoon rice vinegar or apple cider vinegar
- 1 tablespoon honey or sugar
- 2 cloves garlic, minced
- 1 tablespoon sesame oil
- 2 green onions, thinly sliced
- 1 tablespoon vegetable oil, for frying
- Sesame seeds, for garnish
- Optional: sliced green onions for garnish

Instructions:

1. Start by preparing the tofu. Remove it from the package and drain any excess water. Wrap the tofu block in a clean kitchen towel and place a heavy object on top to press out more moisture. Let it sit for about 15-20 minutes.
2. While the tofu is pressing, prepare the sauce. In a small bowl, combine soy sauce, gochujang, rice vinegar, honey or sugar, minced garlic, sesame oil, and thinly sliced green onions. Mix well until all the ingredients are combined and the sugar is dissolved.
3. Once the tofu is pressed, cut it into bite-sized cubes or rectangular pieces, depending on your preference.
4. Heat vegetable oil in a large skillet or frying pan over medium-high heat. Once the oil is hot, add the tofu pieces in a single layer, making sure not to overcrowd the pan. Fry the tofu for 3-4 minutes on each side, or until golden brown and crispy.
5. Once the tofu is cooked, reduce the heat to medium and pour the sauce over the tofu in the pan. Toss gently to coat the tofu evenly with the sauce.
6. Cook for another 2-3 minutes, allowing the sauce to thicken slightly and coat the tofu.
7. Remove the pan from the heat and transfer the pan-fried tofu to a serving dish.
8. Garnish with sesame seeds and sliced green onions, if desired.
9. Serve hot as a side dish or appetizer.

Enjoy the savory, spicy, and slightly sweet flavor of homemade Dubu buchim! Adjust the seasoning according to your taste preferences, and feel free to add more or less gochujang for your desired level of spiciness.

Seasoned perilla leaves (Kkaennip muchim)

Ingredients:

- 20-30 fresh perilla leaves (kkaennip)
- 2 tablespoons soy sauce
- 1 tablespoon sesame oil
- 1 tablespoon rice vinegar or apple cider vinegar
- 1 tablespoon honey or sugar
- 1 clove garlic, minced
- 1 teaspoon sesame seeds
- Optional: sliced green onions for garnish

Instructions:

1. Rinse the perilla leaves under cold water and pat them dry with paper towels. Remove any tough stems.
2. In a small bowl, combine soy sauce, sesame oil, rice vinegar, honey or sugar, minced garlic, and sesame seeds to make the seasoning sauce. Mix well until all the ingredients are combined.
3. Stack the perilla leaves on top of each other and roll them up tightly. Slice the rolled leaves into thin strips crosswise.
4. Place the sliced perilla leaves in a mixing bowl.
5. Pour the seasoning sauce over the perilla leaves and toss well to coat evenly.
6. Let the seasoned perilla leaves marinate in the refrigerator for at least 30 minutes to allow the flavors to meld together.
7. Before serving, garnish the Kkaennip muchim with sliced green onions, if desired.
8. Serve chilled as a side dish with rice and other Korean dishes.

Enjoy the refreshing and flavorful taste of homemade Kkaennip muchim! Adjust the seasoning according to your taste preferences, and feel free to add more or less honey or sugar for your desired level of sweetness.

Pan-fried fish cakes (Eomuk jeon)

Ingredients:

- 200g fish cakes (eomuk), thinly sliced
- 1 egg, beaten
- 2 tablespoons all-purpose flour
- 1 tablespoon vegetable oil
- Soy sauce or dipping sauce, for serving (optional)
- Toasted sesame seeds, for garnish (optional)
- Sliced green onions, for garnish (optional)

Instructions:

1. In a shallow bowl, beat the egg.
2. Place the all-purpose flour on a plate.
3. Heat the vegetable oil in a non-stick skillet or frying pan over medium heat.
4. Dip each slice of fish cake into the beaten egg, then coat it with flour, shaking off any excess.
5. Place the coated fish cake slices in the hot skillet in a single layer, making sure not to overcrowd the pan.
6. Pan-fry the fish cakes for 2-3 minutes on each side, or until golden brown and crispy.
7. Once the fish cakes are cooked through and crispy on both sides, remove them from the skillet and drain on paper towels to remove any excess oil.
8. Repeat the process with the remaining fish cake slices, adding more oil to the skillet if needed.
9. Once all the fish cakes are cooked, transfer them to a serving dish.
10. Serve the pan-fried fish cakes hot as a side dish or snack. You can also serve them with soy sauce or your favorite dipping sauce on the side, and garnish with toasted sesame seeds and sliced green onions, if desired.

Enjoy the savory and crispy taste of homemade Eomuk jeon! Adjust the seasoning according to your taste preferences, and feel free to add other ingredients like chopped vegetables or seasonings to customize the flavor.

Braised potatoes (Gamja jorim)

Ingredients:

- 4 medium potatoes, peeled and cut into chunks
- 2 tablespoons soy sauce
- 1 tablespoon sugar
- 1 tablespoon honey or corn syrup
- 1 tablespoon sesame oil
- 1 cup water or vegetable broth
- 2 cloves garlic, minced
- 1 teaspoon sesame seeds
- Optional: sliced green onions for garnish

Instructions:

1. In a large skillet or pot, combine soy sauce, sugar, honey or corn syrup, sesame oil, minced garlic, and water or vegetable broth. Stir well to combine.
2. Add the potato chunks to the skillet or pot, making sure they are submerged in the liquid.
3. Bring the mixture to a boil over medium-high heat. Once boiling, reduce the heat to low and cover the skillet or pot with a lid.
4. Simmer the potatoes for about 20-25 minutes, or until they are tender and cooked through. Stir occasionally to ensure even cooking and prevent sticking.
5. Once the potatoes are cooked, remove the lid and increase the heat to medium-high. Cook for an additional 5-10 minutes, or until the liquid has thickened and reduced to a glaze, stirring occasionally.
6. Sprinkle sesame seeds over the braised potatoes and toss to coat evenly.
7. Transfer the braised potatoes to a serving dish and garnish with sliced green onions, if desired.
8. Serve hot as a side dish with rice and other Korean dishes.

Enjoy the savory and slightly sweet flavor of homemade Gamja jorim! Adjust the seasoning according to your taste preferences, and feel free to add other ingredients like carrots or onions for extra flavor and texture.

Seasoned dried seaweed (Miyeok muchim)

Ingredients:

- 30g dried seaweed (miyeok)
- 2 tablespoons soy sauce
- 1 tablespoon sesame oil
- 1 tablespoon rice vinegar or apple cider vinegar
- 1 teaspoon sugar
- 1 teaspoon sesame seeds
- 1 clove garlic, minced
- Optional: sliced green onions for garnish

Instructions:

1. Rinse the dried seaweed under cold water to remove any dust or debris. Soak the seaweed in warm water for about 10-15 minutes, or until it becomes soft and pliable. Drain the seaweed and squeeze out any excess water.
2. Cut the soaked seaweed into bite-sized pieces and place them in a mixing bowl.
3. In a small bowl, combine soy sauce, sesame oil, rice vinegar, sugar, minced garlic, and sesame seeds to make the seasoning sauce. Mix well until all the ingredients are combined.
4. Pour the seasoning sauce over the seaweed in the mixing bowl. Toss well to coat the seaweed evenly with the sauce.
5. Let the seasoned seaweed marinate in the refrigerator for at least 30 minutes to allow the flavors to meld together.
6. Before serving, garnish the Miyeok muchim with sliced green onions, if desired.
7. Serve chilled as a side dish with rice and other Korean dishes.

Enjoy the savory and flavorful taste of homemade Miyeok muchim! Adjust the seasoning according to your taste preferences, and feel free to add more or less sugar or garlic for your desired level of sweetness and garlic flavor.

Stir-fried cabbage (Baechu bokkeum)

Ingredients:

- 1/2 head of cabbage, thinly sliced
- 2 cloves garlic, minced
- 1 tablespoon soy sauce
- 1 tablespoon sesame oil
- 1 teaspoon sugar
- 1 teaspoon sesame seeds
- 1 tablespoon vegetable oil, for stir-frying
- Optional: sliced green onions for garnish

Instructions:

1. Heat vegetable oil in a large skillet or wok over medium-high heat.
2. Add minced garlic to the skillet and stir-fry for about 30 seconds, until fragrant.
3. Add the sliced cabbage to the skillet and stir-fry for 3-4 minutes, or until it starts to soften but is still slightly crisp.
4. In a small bowl, mix together soy sauce, sesame oil, sugar, and sesame seeds to make the sauce.
5. Pour the sauce over the stir-fried cabbage in the skillet. Toss gently to coat the cabbage evenly with the sauce.
6. Continue to stir-fry for another 2-3 minutes, until the cabbage is cooked through and the sauce has thickened slightly.
7. Taste the stir-fried cabbage and adjust the seasoning with more soy sauce or sugar, if needed.
8. Remove the skillet from the heat and transfer the stir-fried cabbage to a serving dish.
9. Garnish with sliced green onions, if desired.
10. Serve hot as a side dish with rice and other Korean dishes.

Enjoy the savory and flavorful taste of homemade Baechu bokkeum! Adjust the seasoning according to your taste preferences, and feel free to add other ingredients like carrots or onions for extra flavor and texture.

Seasoned spinach (Sigeumchi-muchim)

Ingredients:

- 1 bunch of spinach (about 300g)
- 2 cloves garlic, minced
- 1 tablespoon soy sauce
- 1 tablespoon sesame oil
- 1 teaspoon sugar
- 1 teaspoon sesame seeds
- Salt, to taste
- Optional: sliced green onions for garnish

Instructions:

1. Wash the spinach thoroughly under cold water to remove any dirt or debris. Trim off any tough stems.
2. Bring a pot of water to a boil. Blanch the spinach in the boiling water for about 1 minute, or until wilted and bright green.
3. Remove the spinach from the boiling water and immediately transfer it to a bowl of ice water to stop the cooking process. Drain the spinach and squeeze out any excess water.
4. In a mixing bowl, combine minced garlic, soy sauce, sesame oil, sugar, and sesame seeds to make the seasoning sauce. Mix well until all the ingredients are combined.
5. Cut the blanched spinach into bite-sized pieces and place them in the mixing bowl with the seasoning sauce. Toss well to coat the spinach evenly with the sauce.
6. Taste the seasoned spinach and adjust the seasoning with salt, if needed.
7. Transfer the seasoned spinach to a serving dish.
8. Garnish with sliced green onions, if desired.
9. Serve the seasoned spinach at room temperature as a side dish with rice and other Korean dishes.

Enjoy the savory and flavorful taste of homemade Sigeumchi-muchim! Adjust the seasoning according to your taste preferences, and feel free to add more or less garlic or sesame oil for your desired level of flavor.

Stir-fried mushrooms (Beoseot bokkeum)

Ingredients:

- 300g mushrooms (such as button mushrooms, shiitake mushrooms, or oyster mushrooms), cleaned and sliced
- 2 cloves garlic, minced
- 1 tablespoon soy sauce
- 1 tablespoon sesame oil
- 1 teaspoon sugar
- 1 teaspoon sesame seeds
- 1 tablespoon vegetable oil, for stir-frying
- Optional: sliced green onions for garnish

Instructions:

1. Heat vegetable oil in a large skillet or wok over medium-high heat.
2. Add minced garlic to the skillet and stir-fry for about 30 seconds, until fragrant.
3. Add the sliced mushrooms to the skillet and stir-fry for 4-5 minutes, or until they start to soften and release their moisture.
4. In a small bowl, mix together soy sauce, sesame oil, sugar, and sesame seeds to make the sauce.
5. Pour the sauce over the stir-fried mushrooms in the skillet. Toss gently to coat the mushrooms evenly with the sauce.
6. Continue to stir-fry for another 2-3 minutes, until the mushrooms are cooked through and the sauce has thickened slightly.
7. Taste the stir-fried mushrooms and adjust the seasoning with more soy sauce or sugar, if needed.
8. Remove the skillet from the heat and transfer the stir-fried mushrooms to a serving dish.
9. Garnish with sliced green onions, if desired.
10. Serve hot as a side dish with rice and other Korean dishes.

Enjoy the savory and flavorful taste of homemade Beoseot bokkeum! Adjust the seasoning according to your taste preferences, and feel free to add other ingredients like bell peppers or onions for extra flavor and texture.

Braised dried anchovies (Myeolchi jorim)

Ingredients:

- 1 cup dried anchovies (myeolchi), heads and guts removed
- 2 tablespoons soy sauce
- 1 tablespoon sugar
- 1 tablespoon honey or corn syrup
- 1 tablespoon sesame oil
- 1 tablespoon rice wine or water
- 2 cloves garlic, minced
- 1 teaspoon sesame seeds

Instructions:

1. Rinse the dried anchovies under cold water to remove any impurities. Pat them dry with paper towels.
2. In a medium-sized pot, combine soy sauce, sugar, honey or corn syrup, sesame oil, rice wine or water, and minced garlic. Stir well to combine.
3. Add the dried anchovies to the pot and stir to coat them evenly with the sauce.
4. Bring the mixture to a simmer over medium heat.
5. Once simmering, reduce the heat to low and cover the pot with a lid. Let it cook for about 15-20 minutes, stirring occasionally, until the anchovies are tender and the sauce has thickened slightly.
6. Taste the braised anchovies and adjust the seasoning if needed, adding more sugar or soy sauce to taste.
7. Once the anchovies are cooked through and the sauce has thickened to your liking, remove the pot from the heat.
8. Sprinkle sesame seeds over the braised anchovies and toss gently to coat.
9. Transfer the braised anchovies to a serving dish and serve hot or at room temperature as a side dish or snack.

Enjoy the savory and slightly sweet flavor of homemade Myeolchi jorim! Adjust the seasoning according to your taste preferences, and feel free to add more or less honey or sugar for your desired level of sweetness.

Seasoned radish salad (Musaengchae)

Ingredients:

- 1 large Korean radish (mu) or daikon radish
- 2 tablespoons rice vinegar or apple cider vinegar
- 2 tablespoons sugar
- 1 teaspoon salt
- 1 teaspoon sesame oil
- 1 teaspoon sesame seeds
- 2 cloves garlic, minced
- Optional: sliced green onions for garnish

Instructions:

1. Peel the radish and rinse it under cold water. Use a mandoline slicer or a sharp knife to julienne the radish into thin strips. Place the julienned radish in a large mixing bowl.
2. In a small bowl, mix together rice vinegar, sugar, salt, sesame oil, minced garlic, and sesame seeds to make the seasoning sauce. Mix well until all the ingredients are combined.
3. Pour the seasoning sauce over the julienned radish in the mixing bowl. Toss well to coat the radish evenly with the sauce.
4. Let the radish marinate in the refrigerator for at least 30 minutes to allow the flavors to meld together.
5. Before serving, garnish the Musaengchae with sliced green onions, if desired.
6. Serve chilled as a side dish with rice and other Korean dishes.

Enjoy the tangy and refreshing flavor of homemade Musaengchae! Adjust the seasoning according to your taste preferences, and feel free to add more or less sugar or garlic for your desired level of sweetness and garlic flavor.

Pan-fried pancakes with vegetables (Pajeon)

Ingredients:

- 1 cup all-purpose flour
- 1 cup water
- 2 eggs
- 2 cups mixed vegetables (such as green onions, carrots, zucchini, and/or bell peppers), thinly sliced
- 1/2 cup seafood (such as shrimp or squid), optional
- 2 tablespoons soy sauce
- 1 tablespoon sesame oil
- 1 tablespoon vegetable oil, for frying
- Salt and pepper, to taste
- Optional: sliced green onions for garnish

Instructions:

1. In a large mixing bowl, combine all-purpose flour, water, and eggs. Whisk until smooth to make the pancake batter.
2. Add mixed vegetables and seafood (if using) to the pancake batter. Mix well to combine.
3. Season the batter with soy sauce, sesame oil, salt, and pepper. Mix again until all the ingredients are evenly distributed.
4. Heat vegetable oil in a large non-stick skillet or frying pan over medium heat.
5. Once the oil is hot, pour a ladleful of the pancake batter into the skillet, spreading it out into a thin, even layer.
6. Cook the pancake for 3-4 minutes on each side, or until golden brown and crispy. Use a spatula to flip the pancake halfway through cooking.
7. Repeat the process with the remaining pancake batter, adding more oil to the skillet as needed.
8. Once all the pancakes are cooked, transfer them to a serving platter.
9. Garnish the Pajeon with sliced green onions, if desired.
10. Serve hot as an appetizer or side dish with dipping sauce (such as soy sauce mixed with vinegar and/or sesame oil) on the side.

Enjoy the savory and crispy taste of homemade Pajeon! Feel free to customize the vegetables and seafood according to your preferences, and adjust the seasoning to suit your taste.

Stir-fried shredded squid (Ojingeo bokkeum)

Ingredients:

- 200g dried shredded squid
- 2 tablespoons soy sauce
- 1 tablespoon sesame oil
- 1 tablespoon gochugaru (Korean red pepper flakes)
- 1 tablespoon sugar
- 1 tablespoon vegetable oil
- 2 cloves garlic, minced
- 1 teaspoon sesame seeds
- Optional: sliced green onions for garnish

Instructions:

1. Rinse the dried shredded squid under cold water to remove any impurities. Soak it in warm water for about 10-15 minutes, or until it becomes soft. Drain and squeeze out any excess water.
2. In a small bowl, mix together soy sauce, sesame oil, gochugaru, and sugar to make the sauce.
3. Heat vegetable oil in a large skillet or wok over medium-high heat.
4. Add minced garlic to the skillet and stir-fry for about 30 seconds, until fragrant.
5. Add the softened shredded squid to the skillet and stir-fry for 2-3 minutes.
6. Pour the sauce over the squid in the skillet. Toss gently to coat the squid evenly with the sauce.
7. Continue to stir-fry for another 2-3 minutes, until the squid is heated through and the sauce has thickened slightly.
8. Sprinkle sesame seeds over the stir-fried squid and toss gently to coat.
9. Transfer the Ojingeo bokkeum to a serving dish.
10. Garnish with sliced green onions, if desired.
11. Serve hot as a side dish with rice and other Korean dishes.

Enjoy the savory and spicy flavor of homemade Ojingeo bokkeum! Adjust the amount of gochugaru according to your desired level of spiciness, and feel free to add more or less sugar for your preferred level of sweetness.

Braised burdock roots (Ueong jorim)

Ingredients:

- 200g burdock roots
- 2 tablespoons soy sauce
- 1 tablespoon sugar
- 1 tablespoon sesame oil
- 1 tablespoon sesame seeds
- 1 cup water
- 2 cloves garlic, minced
- Optional: sliced green onions for garnish

Instructions:

1. Peel the burdock roots and cut them into thin strips or matchsticks.
2. In a medium-sized pot, combine soy sauce, sugar, sesame oil, sesame seeds, water, and minced garlic. Stir well to combine.
3. Add the sliced burdock roots to the pot and stir to coat them evenly with the sauce.
4. Bring the mixture to a boil over medium-high heat.
5. Once boiling, reduce the heat to low and cover the pot with a lid. Let it simmer for about 20-25 minutes, or until the burdock roots are tender and the sauce has thickened slightly. Stir occasionally to prevent sticking.
6. Once the burdock roots are cooked through and the sauce has thickened to your liking, remove the pot from the heat.
7. Transfer the braised burdock roots to a serving dish.
8. Garnish with sliced green onions, if desired.
9. Serve hot or at room temperature as a side dish with rice and other Korean dishes.

Enjoy the savory and flavorful taste of homemade Ueong jorim! Adjust the seasoning according to your taste preferences, and feel free to add more or less sugar or sesame oil for your desired level of sweetness and flavor.

Seasoned mung bean sprouts (Sukju namul)

Ingredients:

- 300g mung bean sprouts
- 1 tablespoon sesame oil
- 1 tablespoon soy sauce
- 1 clove garlic, minced
- 1 teaspoon sesame seeds
- Salt, to taste
- Optional: sliced green onions for garnish

Instructions:

1. Rinse the mung bean sprouts under cold water to remove any impurities. Drain them well.
2. In a large pot, bring water to a boil. Add the mung bean sprouts to the boiling water and blanch them for about 1-2 minutes.
3. Remove the mung bean sprouts from the boiling water and immediately transfer them to a bowl of ice water to stop the cooking process. Drain the sprouts well and squeeze out any excess water.
4. In a mixing bowl, combine sesame oil, soy sauce, minced garlic, sesame seeds, and salt to taste. Mix well to make the seasoning sauce.
5. Add the blanched mung bean sprouts to the mixing bowl with the seasoning sauce. Toss well to coat the sprouts evenly with the sauce.
6. Let the seasoned mung bean sprouts marinate in the refrigerator for at least 30 minutes to allow the flavors to meld together.
7. Before serving, garnish the Sukju namul with sliced green onions, if desired.
8. Serve chilled or at room temperature as a side dish with rice and other Korean dishes.

Enjoy the fresh and flavorful taste of homemade Sukju namul! Adjust the seasoning according to your taste preferences, and feel free to add more garlic or sesame oil for extra flavor.

Steamed egg custard (Gyeran jjim)

Ingredients:

- 3 large eggs
- 1 cup water or chicken broth
- 1 tablespoon soy sauce
- 1 teaspoon sesame oil
- 1 teaspoon salt
- 1 green onion, thinly sliced (optional)
- Sesame seeds, for garnish (optional)

Instructions:

1. In a mixing bowl, beat the eggs until well combined.
2. Add water or chicken broth, soy sauce, sesame oil, salt, and sliced green onion (if using) to the eggs. Mix well to combine.
3. Strain the egg mixture through a fine-mesh sieve into a heatproof bowl. This will help to remove any foam and ensure a smooth texture.
4. Cover the bowl with aluminum foil or plastic wrap.
5. Prepare a steamer by bringing water to a boil over medium-high heat.
6. Once the water is boiling, reduce the heat to medium-low. Place the covered bowl of egg mixture in the steamer basket.
7. Steam the egg custard for about 10-15 minutes, or until it is set and no longer jiggly in the center. To check for doneness, insert a toothpick into the center of the custard—if it comes out clean, the custard is ready.
8. Once cooked, carefully remove the bowl from the steamer using oven mitts or kitchen towels.
9. Garnish the steamed egg custard with sesame seeds, if desired.
10. Serve hot as a side dish or appetizer with rice and other Korean dishes.

Enjoy the creamy and comforting taste of homemade Gyeran jjim! Feel free to customize the dish by adding other ingredients such as chopped vegetables or seafood according to your preferences.

Stir-fried soybean sprouts (Kongnamul bokkeum)

Ingredients:

- 300g soybean sprouts (kongnamul)
- 2 cloves garlic, minced
- 1 tablespoon vegetable oil
- 1 tablespoon soy sauce
- 1 teaspoon sesame oil
- 1 teaspoon sesame seeds
- Salt, to taste
- Optional: sliced green onions for garnish

Instructions:

1. Rinse the soybean sprouts under cold water to remove any impurities. Drain them well.
2. Heat vegetable oil in a large skillet or wok over medium-high heat.
3. Add minced garlic to the skillet and stir-fry for about 30 seconds, until fragrant.
4. Add the soybean sprouts to the skillet and stir-fry for 3-4 minutes, or until they start to soften.
5. Drizzle soy sauce and sesame oil over the stir-fried soybean sprouts. Toss gently to coat them evenly with the sauce.
6. Continue to stir-fry for another 2-3 minutes, until the soybean sprouts are cooked through but still crisp.
7. Season with salt to taste and sprinkle sesame seeds over the stir-fried soybean sprouts. Toss gently to combine.
8. Transfer the Kongnamul bokkeum to a serving dish.
9. Garnish with sliced green onions, if desired.
10. Serve hot or at room temperature as a side dish with rice and other Korean dishes.

Enjoy the savory and crunchy taste of homemade Kongnamul bokkeum! Adjust the seasoning according to your taste preferences, and feel free to add other ingredients like carrots or bell peppers for extra flavor and texture.

Pan-fried tofu with soy sauce (Dubu ganjangjorim)

Ingredients:

- 1 block firm tofu
- 2 tablespoons soy sauce
- 1 tablespoon sesame oil
- 1 tablespoon rice vinegar or apple cider vinegar
- 1 tablespoon sugar
- 2 cloves garlic, minced
- 1 teaspoon sesame seeds
- 1 tablespoon vegetable oil, for frying
- Optional: sliced green onions for garnish

Instructions:

1. Slice the tofu into rectangular pieces, about 1/4 inch thick.
2. In a small bowl, mix together soy sauce, sesame oil, rice vinegar or apple cider vinegar, sugar, minced garlic, and sesame seeds to make the marinade.
3. Place the tofu slices in a shallow dish and pour the marinade over them. Make sure the tofu is well coated with the marinade. Let it marinate for at least 15-20 minutes to absorb the flavors.
4. Heat vegetable oil in a large skillet or frying pan over medium-high heat.
5. Once the oil is hot, add the marinated tofu slices to the skillet. Be careful not to overcrowd the skillet; you may need to cook the tofu in batches.
6. Cook the tofu for about 3-4 minutes on each side, or until golden brown and crispy.
7. Once the tofu is cooked through and crispy on both sides, remove it from the skillet and transfer to a serving dish.
8. Garnish with sliced green onions, if desired.
9. Serve hot as a side dish with rice and other Korean dishes.

Enjoy the savory and flavorful taste of homemade Dubu ganjangjorim! Adjust the seasoning according to your taste preferences, and feel free to add more or less garlic or sesame oil for your desired level of flavor.

Spicy stir-fried squid (Ojingeo bokkeum)

Ingredients:

- 300g squid tubes, cleaned and sliced into rings
- 2 tablespoons gochujang (Korean red pepper paste)
- 1 tablespoon soy sauce
- 1 tablespoon sesame oil
- 1 tablespoon sugar
- 2 cloves garlic, minced
- 1 teaspoon sesame seeds
- 1 tablespoon vegetable oil
- Optional: sliced green onions for garnish

Instructions:

1. In a small bowl, mix together gochujang, soy sauce, sesame oil, sugar, minced garlic, and sesame seeds to make the marinade.
2. Place the sliced squid rings in a mixing bowl and pour the marinade over them. Toss well to coat the squid evenly with the marinade. Let it marinate for at least 15-20 minutes to absorb the flavors.
3. Heat vegetable oil in a large skillet or wok over medium-high heat.
4. Once the oil is hot, add the marinated squid to the skillet. Stir-fry for about 3-4 minutes, or until the squid is cooked through and the sauce has thickened slightly.
5. Be careful not to overcook the squid, as it can become tough and rubbery.
6. Once the squid is cooked through and the sauce has thickened, remove the skillet from the heat.
7. Transfer the spicy stir-fried squid to a serving dish.
8. Garnish with sliced green onions, if desired.
9. Serve hot as a main dish or as a side dish with rice and other Korean dishes.

Enjoy the spicy and flavorful taste of homemade Ojingeo bokkeum! Adjust the amount of gochujang according to your desired level of spiciness, and feel free to add more or less sugar for your preferred level of sweetness.

Braised lotus root with soy sauce (Yeonkeun jangajji)

Ingredients:

- 2 lotus roots, peeled and thinly sliced
- 2 cups water
- 1/4 cup soy sauce
- 2 tablespoons rice vinegar or apple cider vinegar
- 2 tablespoons sugar
- 2 cloves garlic, minced
- 1 teaspoon sesame oil
- 1 teaspoon sesame seeds
- Optional: sliced green onions for garnish

Instructions:

1. In a large pot, combine water, soy sauce, rice vinegar or apple cider vinegar, sugar, minced garlic, sesame oil, and sesame seeds. Stir well to combine.
2. Add the sliced lotus roots to the pot and stir to coat them evenly with the sauce.
3. Bring the mixture to a boil over medium-high heat.
4. Once boiling, reduce the heat to low and cover the pot with a lid. Let it simmer for about 20-25 minutes, or until the lotus roots are tender.
5. Stir the lotus roots occasionally to ensure even cooking and absorption of the sauce.
6. Once the lotus roots are cooked through and the sauce has thickened slightly, remove the pot from the heat.
7. Transfer the braised lotus roots to a serving dish.
8. Garnish with sliced green onions, if desired.
9. Serve hot or at room temperature as a side dish with rice and other Korean dishes.

Enjoy the savory and flavorful taste of homemade Yeonkeun jangajji! Adjust the seasoning according to your taste preferences, and feel free to add more or less sugar or vinegar for your desired level of sweetness and acidity.

Seasoned perilla seeds (Deulkkae jangajji)

Ingredients:

- 1 cup perilla seeds (deulkkae)
- 2 cups water
- 1/4 cup soy sauce
- 2 tablespoons rice vinegar or apple cider vinegar
- 2 tablespoons sugar
- 2 cloves garlic, minced
- 1 teaspoon sesame oil
- 1 teaspoon sesame seeds
- Optional: sliced green onions for garnish

Instructions:

1. In a small pot, bring water to a boil over medium-high heat.
2. Add perilla seeds to the boiling water and blanch them for about 1 minute.
3. Drain the blanched perilla seeds and transfer them to a mixing bowl.
4. In the same pot, combine soy sauce, rice vinegar or apple cider vinegar, sugar, minced garlic, sesame oil, and sesame seeds. Stir well to combine.
5. Pour the sauce over the blanched perilla seeds in the mixing bowl. Toss well to coat the seeds evenly with the sauce.
6. Let the seasoned perilla seeds marinate for at least 30 minutes to allow the flavors to meld together.
7. Before serving, garnish the Deulkkae jangajji with sliced green onions, if desired.
8. Serve chilled or at room temperature as a side dish or snack.

Enjoy the savory and flavorful taste of homemade Deulkkae jangajji! Adjust the seasoning according to your taste preferences, and feel free to add more or less sugar or vinegar for your desired level of sweetness and acidity.

Braised dried radish greens (Mu saengchae jorim)

Ingredients:

- 200g dried radish greens (mu saengchae)
- 2 cups water
- 2 tablespoons soy sauce
- 1 tablespoon sesame oil
- 1 tablespoon sugar
- 2 cloves garlic, minced
- 1 teaspoon sesame seeds
- Optional: sliced green onions for garnish

Instructions:

1. Rinse the dried radish greens under cold water to remove any impurities. Soak them in warm water for about 10-15 minutes, or until they become soft. Drain and squeeze out any excess water.
2. In a medium-sized pot, combine water, soy sauce, sesame oil, sugar, minced garlic, and sesame seeds. Stir well to combine.
3. Add the softened radish greens to the pot and stir to coat them evenly with the sauce.
4. Bring the mixture to a boil over medium-high heat.
5. Once boiling, reduce the heat to low and cover the pot with a lid. Let it simmer for about 15-20 minutes, stirring occasionally, until the radish greens are tender and the sauce has thickened slightly.
6. Once the radish greens are cooked through and the sauce has thickened to your liking, remove the pot from the heat.
7. Transfer the braised radish greens to a serving dish.
8. Garnish with sliced green onions, if desired.
9. Serve hot or at room temperature as a side dish with rice and other Korean dishes.

Enjoy the savory and flavorful taste of homemade Mu saengchae jorim! Adjust the seasoning according to your taste preferences, and feel free to add more or less sugar or soy sauce for your desired level of sweetness and saltiness.

Stir-fried shredded dried squid (Ojingeochae bokkeum)

Ingredients:

- 200g dried shredded squid (ojingeochae)
- 2 tablespoons soy sauce
- 1 tablespoon sesame oil
- 1 tablespoon sugar
- 2 cloves garlic, minced
- 1 teaspoon sesame seeds
- 1 tablespoon vegetable oil
- Optional: sliced green onions for garnish

Instructions:

1. Rinse the dried shredded squid under cold water to remove any impurities. Soak them in warm water for about 10-15 minutes, or until they become soft. Drain and squeeze out any excess water.
2. In a small bowl, mix together soy sauce, sesame oil, sugar, minced garlic, and sesame seeds to make the sauce.
3. Heat vegetable oil in a large skillet or frying pan over medium-high heat.
4. Add the softened shredded squid to the skillet and stir-fry for about 3-4 minutes.
5. Pour the sauce over the squid in the skillet. Toss gently to coat the squid evenly with the sauce.
6. Continue to stir-fry for another 2-3 minutes, until the squid is heated through and the sauce has thickened slightly.
7. Once cooked, remove the skillet from the heat.
8. Transfer the Ojingeochae bokkeum to a serving dish.
9. Garnish with sliced green onions, if desired.
10. Serve hot or at room temperature as a side dish or snack.

Enjoy the savory and chewy taste of homemade Ojingeochae bokkeum! Adjust the seasoning according to your taste preferences, and feel free to add more or less sugar or garlic for your desired level of sweetness and flavor.

Spicy stir-fried pork belly (Dwaeji bulgogi)

Ingredients:

- 500g pork belly, thinly sliced
- 3 tablespoons gochujang (Korean red pepper paste)
- 2 tablespoons soy sauce
- 1 tablespoon sesame oil
- 1 tablespoon honey or sugar
- 1 tablespoon rice wine (mirin) or rice vinegar
- 2 cloves garlic, minced
- 1 teaspoon ginger, minced
- 1 onion, thinly sliced
- 2 green onions, chopped
- 1 tablespoon vegetable oil
- Sesame seeds, for garnish
- Optional: sliced carrots, bell peppers, or mushrooms for added vegetables

Instructions:

1. In a bowl, mix together the gochujang, soy sauce, sesame oil, honey or sugar, rice wine or rice vinegar, minced garlic, and minced ginger to make the marinade.
2. Add the sliced pork belly to the marinade and mix well to coat. Let it marinate for at least 30 minutes, or overnight in the refrigerator for best results.
3. Heat vegetable oil in a large skillet or wok over medium-high heat.
4. Add the marinated pork belly to the skillet, along with the sliced onion. Stir-fry for 5-7 minutes, or until the pork is cooked through and caramelized.
5. If using additional vegetables, add them to the skillet and stir-fry for an additional 3-4 minutes, or until they are tender-crisp.
6. Garnish the spicy stir-fried pork belly with chopped green onions and sesame seeds.
7. Serve hot with steamed rice and your favorite Korean side dishes.

Enjoy the spicy and savory flavor of homemade Dwaeji bulgogi! Adjust the amount of gochujang according to your desired level of spiciness, and feel free to add more vegetables for extra flavor and nutrition.

Stir-fried spicy octopus (Nakji bokkeum)

Ingredients:

- 500g baby octopus, cleaned
- 2 tablespoons gochujang (Korean red pepper paste)
- 1 tablespoon soy sauce
- 1 tablespoon sesame oil
- 1 tablespoon honey or sugar
- 1 tablespoon rice wine (mirin) or rice vinegar
- 2 cloves garlic, minced
- 1 teaspoon ginger, minced
- 1 onion, thinly sliced
- 2 green onions, chopped
- 1 tablespoon vegetable oil
- Sesame seeds, for garnish
- Optional: sliced carrots, bell peppers, or mushrooms for added vegetables

Instructions:

1. In a bowl, mix together the gochujang, soy sauce, sesame oil, honey or sugar, rice wine or rice vinegar, minced garlic, and minced ginger to make the marinade.
2. Add the cleaned baby octopus to the marinade and mix well to coat. Let it marinate for at least 30 minutes, or overnight in the refrigerator for best results.
3. Heat vegetable oil in a large skillet or wok over medium-high heat.
4. Add the marinated baby octopus to the skillet, along with the sliced onion. Stir-fry for 5-7 minutes, or until the octopus is cooked through and caramelized.
5. If using additional vegetables, add them to the skillet and stir-fry for an additional 3-4 minutes, or until they are tender-crisp.
6. Garnish the spicy stir-fried octopus with chopped green onions and sesame seeds.
7. Serve hot with steamed rice and your favorite Korean side dishes.

Enjoy the spicy and flavorful taste of homemade Nakji bokkeum! Adjust the amount of gochujang according to your desired level of spiciness, and feel free to add more vegetables for extra flavor and nutrition.

Seasoned dried pollack (Bugeo muchim)

Ingredients:

- 200g dried pollack (bugeo)
- 2 cups water
- 2 tablespoons soy sauce
- 1 tablespoon sesame oil
- 1 tablespoon rice vinegar or apple cider vinegar
- 1 tablespoon sugar
- 2 cloves garlic, minced
- 1 teaspoon sesame seeds
- 1 tablespoon green onions, thinly sliced (optional)

Instructions:

1. Rinse the dried pollack under cold water to remove any impurities. Soak them in warm water for about 10-15 minutes, or until they become soft. Drain and squeeze out any excess water.
2. In a small pot, combine water, soy sauce, sesame oil, rice vinegar or apple cider vinegar, sugar, minced garlic, and sesame seeds. Stir well to combine.
3. Add the softened dried pollack to the pot and stir to coat them evenly with the sauce.
4. Bring the mixture to a boil over medium-high heat.
5. Once boiling, reduce the heat to low and cover the pot with a lid. Let it simmer for about 10-15 minutes, stirring occasionally, until the dried pollack is tender and the sauce has thickened slightly.
6. Once cooked, remove the pot from the heat.
7. Transfer the seasoned dried pollack to a serving dish.
8. Garnish with thinly sliced green onions, if desired.
9. Serve hot or at room temperature as a side dish with rice and other Korean dishes.

Enjoy the savory and flavorful taste of homemade Bugeo muchim! Adjust the seasoning according to your taste preferences, and feel free to add more or less sugar or vinegar for your desired level of sweetness and acidity.

Pan-fried tofu with spicy sauce (Dubu buchim-yangnyeom)

Ingredients:

For the tofu:

- 1 block firm tofu, drained and sliced into rectangles or triangles
- 2 tablespoons vegetable oil

For the spicy sauce:

- 2 tablespoons soy sauce
- 1 tablespoon gochujang (Korean red pepper paste)
- 1 tablespoon honey or sugar
- 1 tablespoon sesame oil
- 2 cloves garlic, minced
- 1 teaspoon rice vinegar or apple cider vinegar
- 1 teaspoon sesame seeds
- Optional: sliced green onions for garnish

Instructions:

1. In a small bowl, whisk together soy sauce, gochujang, honey or sugar, sesame oil, minced garlic, rice vinegar or apple cider vinegar, and sesame seeds to make the spicy sauce. Set aside.
2. Heat vegetable oil in a large skillet or non-stick pan over medium-high heat.
3. Carefully add the sliced tofu to the skillet and pan-fry for about 4-5 minutes on each side, or until golden brown and crispy.
4. Once the tofu is cooked and crispy, reduce the heat to low and pour the spicy sauce over the tofu in the skillet.
5. Gently toss the tofu in the spicy sauce until evenly coated. Allow the sauce to simmer for 1-2 minutes, stirring occasionally, until it thickens slightly.
6. Once the sauce has thickened and the tofu is well coated, remove the skillet from the heat.
7. Transfer the pan-fried tofu with spicy sauce to a serving dish.

8. Garnish with sliced green onions, if desired.
9. Serve hot as a main dish or appetizer with rice and your favorite Korean side dishes.

Enjoy the deliciously spicy and flavorful taste of homemade Dubu buchim-yangnyeom! Adjust the amount of gochujang according to your desired level of spiciness, and feel free to add more or less honey or sugar for your preferred level of sweetness.

Stir-fried dried anchovies with peanuts (Kongari-myeolchi bokkeum)

Ingredients:

- 1 cup dried anchovies (myeolchi), heads and guts removed
- 1/2 cup peanuts
- 2 tablespoons soy sauce
- 1 tablespoon honey or sugar
- 1 tablespoon sesame oil
- 2 cloves garlic, minced
- 1 teaspoon sesame seeds
- 1 tablespoon vegetable oil

Instructions:

1. Rinse the dried anchovies under cold water to remove any impurities. Drain well and pat them dry with paper towels.
2. In a small bowl, mix together soy sauce, honey or sugar, sesame oil, minced garlic, and sesame seeds to make the sauce. Set aside.
3. Heat vegetable oil in a large skillet or non-stick pan over medium heat.
4. Add the dried anchovies to the skillet and stir-fry for 2-3 minutes, or until they are lightly browned and crispy.
5. Add the peanuts to the skillet and continue to stir-fry for another 2-3 minutes, until the peanuts are toasted and fragrant.
6. Pour the sauce over the dried anchovies and peanuts in the skillet. Stir well to coat them evenly with the sauce.
7. Continue to stir-fry for another 1-2 minutes, or until the sauce has thickened slightly and coats the anchovies and peanuts.
8. Once cooked, remove the skillet from the heat.
9. Transfer the stir-fried dried anchovies with peanuts to a serving dish.
10. Serve hot or at room temperature as a side dish or snack.

Enjoy the savory and crunchy taste of homemade Kongari-myeolchi bokkeum! Adjust the seasoning according to your taste preferences, and feel free to add more or less honey or sugar for your desired level of sweetness.

Spicy cucumber salad with vinegar (Oi-muchim)

Ingredients:

- 2 medium cucumbers, thinly sliced
- 1/4 cup rice vinegar or apple cider vinegar
- 2 tablespoons soy sauce
- 1 tablespoon sesame oil
- 1 tablespoon sugar
- 1 clove garlic, minced
- 1 teaspoon gochugaru (Korean red pepper flakes) or chili flakes
- 1 teaspoon sesame seeds
- Optional: thinly sliced green onions or cilantro for garnish

Instructions:

1. In a small bowl, mix together rice vinegar or apple cider vinegar, soy sauce, sesame oil, sugar, minced garlic, gochugaru or chili flakes, and sesame seeds to make the dressing.
2. Place the thinly sliced cucumbers in a large mixing bowl.
3. Pour the dressing over the cucumbers in the bowl. Toss well to coat the cucumbers evenly with the dressing.
4. Let the cucumber salad marinate in the refrigerator for at least 30 minutes to allow the flavors to meld together.
5. Before serving, garnish the Oi-muchim with thinly sliced green onions or cilantro, if desired.
6. Serve cold as a refreshing side dish with rice and other Korean dishes.

Enjoy the tangy and spicy taste of homemade Oi-muchim! Adjust the amount of gochugaru or chili flakes according to your desired level of spiciness, and feel free to add more or less sugar for your preferred level of sweetness.

Stir-fried fish cake with vegetables (Eomuk bokkeum)

Ingredients:

- 200g fish cake (eomuk), thinly sliced
- 1/2 onion, thinly sliced
- 1 carrot, julienned
- 1/2 red bell pepper, thinly sliced
- 1/2 green bell pepper, thinly sliced
- 2 cloves garlic, minced
- 2 tablespoons soy sauce
- 1 tablespoon sesame oil
- 1 tablespoon gochujang (Korean red pepper paste)
- 1 teaspoon sugar
- 1 teaspoon sesame seeds
- 1 tablespoon vegetable oil

Instructions:

1. Heat vegetable oil in a large skillet or wok over medium-high heat.
2. Add the thinly sliced fish cake to the skillet and stir-fry for 2-3 minutes, or until lightly browned and heated through. Remove from the skillet and set aside.
3. In the same skillet, add a little more vegetable oil if needed. Add the minced garlic and stir-fry for about 30 seconds, or until fragrant.
4. Add the sliced onion, carrot, and bell peppers to the skillet. Stir-fry for 3-4 minutes, or until the vegetables are tender-crisp.
5. In a small bowl, mix together soy sauce, sesame oil, gochujang, sugar, and sesame seeds to make the sauce.
6. Add the cooked fish cake back to the skillet with the vegetables.
7. Pour the sauce over the fish cake and vegetables in the skillet. Stir well to coat them evenly with the sauce.
8. Continue to stir-fry for another 1-2 minutes, or until the sauce has thickened slightly and coats the fish cake and vegetables.
9. Once cooked, remove the skillet from the heat.
10. Transfer the stir-fried fish cake with vegetables to a serving dish.
11. Serve hot as a main dish or as a side dish with rice and other Korean dishes.

Enjoy the savory and flavorful taste of homemade Eomuk bokkeum! Adjust the amount of gochujang according to your desired level of spiciness, and feel free to add more vegetables or substitute with your favorites.

Stir-fried dried anchovies with peanuts (Kongari-myeolchi bokkeum)

Ingredients:

- 1 cup dried anchovies (myeolchi), heads and guts removed
- 1/2 cup peanuts
- 2 tablespoons soy sauce
- 1 tablespoon honey or sugar
- 1 tablespoon sesame oil
- 2 cloves garlic, minced
- 1 teaspoon sesame seeds
- 1 tablespoon vegetable oil

Instructions:

1. Rinse the dried anchovies under cold water to remove any impurities. Drain well and pat them dry with paper towels.
2. Heat vegetable oil in a large skillet or non-stick pan over medium heat.
3. Add the dried anchovies to the skillet and stir-fry for 2-3 minutes, or until they are lightly browned and crispy.
4. Add the peanuts to the skillet and continue to stir-fry for another 2-3 minutes, until the peanuts are toasted and fragrant.
5. In a small bowl, mix together soy sauce, honey or sugar, sesame oil, minced garlic, and sesame seeds to make the sauce.
6. Pour the sauce over the dried anchovies and peanuts in the skillet. Stir well to coat them evenly with the sauce.
7. Continue to stir-fry for another 1-2 minutes, or until the sauce has thickened slightly and coats the anchovies and peanuts.
8. Once cooked, remove the skillet from the heat.
9. Transfer the stir-fried dried anchovies with peanuts to a serving dish.
10. Serve hot or at room temperature as a side dish or snack.

Enjoy the savory and crunchy taste of homemade Kongari-myeolchi bokkeum! Adjust the seasoning according to your taste preferences, and feel free to add more honey or sugar for your desired level of sweetness.

Seasoned burdock roots (Ueong muchim)

Ingredients:

- 200g burdock roots (ueong), peeled and julienned
- 1 tablespoon soy sauce
- 1 tablespoon sesame oil
- 1 tablespoon rice vinegar or apple cider vinegar
- 1 teaspoon sugar
- 1 clove garlic, minced
- 1 teaspoon sesame seeds
- Optional: thinly sliced green onions for garnish

Instructions:

1. Peel the burdock roots and julienne them into thin strips.
2. In a pot of boiling water, blanch the julienned burdock roots for about 3-4 minutes, or until they are tender. Drain and rinse them under cold water to stop the cooking process. Drain well and pat them dry with paper towels.
3. In a small bowl, mix together soy sauce, sesame oil, rice vinegar or apple cider vinegar, sugar, minced garlic, and sesame seeds to make the dressing.
4. Place the blanched burdock roots in a mixing bowl.
5. Pour the dressing over the burdock roots in the bowl. Toss well to coat the burdock roots evenly with the dressing.
6. Let the seasoned burdock roots marinate in the refrigerator for at least 30 minutes to allow the flavors to meld together.
7. Before serving, garnish the Ueong muchim with thinly sliced green onions, if desired.
8. Serve cold as a side dish with rice and other Korean dishes.

Enjoy the savory and flavorful taste of homemade Ueong muchim! Adjust the seasoning according to your taste preferences, and feel free to add more or less sugar or vinegar for your desired level of sweetness and acidity.

Pan-fried fish cakes with egg batter (Eomuk jeon)

Ingredients:

- 200g fish cakes (eomuk), sliced into bite-sized pieces
- 2 eggs
- 2 tablespoons all-purpose flour
- 1 tablespoon vegetable oil
- Salt and pepper to taste
- Optional: thinly sliced green onions for garnish

Instructions:

1. In a mixing bowl, crack the eggs and beat them lightly. Season with a pinch of salt and pepper.
2. Add the all-purpose flour to the beaten eggs and mix until well combined. The batter should have a smooth consistency.
3. Heat the vegetable oil in a non-stick skillet or frying pan over medium heat.
4. Dip each piece of fish cake into the egg batter, ensuring that it's fully coated.
5. Carefully place the coated fish cakes in the heated skillet. Cook for 2-3 minutes on each side, or until golden brown and crispy.
6. Once the fish cakes are cooked through and crispy on the outside, transfer them to a plate lined with paper towels to drain any excess oil.
7. Repeat the process with the remaining fish cakes and egg batter.
8. Garnish the pan-fried fish cakes with thinly sliced green onions, if desired.
9. Serve hot as a snack or appetizer, accompanied by your favorite dipping sauce or enjoyed on their own.

Enjoy the crispy and flavorful taste of homemade Eomuk jeon! Feel free to customize the seasoning according to your taste preferences, and experiment with different dipping sauces for added flavor.

Stir-fried shredded dried squid with vegetables (Ojingeochae bokkeum)

Ingredients:

- 100g dried shredded squid (ojingeochae)
- 1 carrot, julienned
- 1 onion, thinly sliced
- 1 red bell pepper, thinly sliced
- 1 green bell pepper, thinly sliced
- 2 cloves garlic, minced
- 2 tablespoons soy sauce
- 1 tablespoon sesame oil
- 1 tablespoon honey or sugar
- 1 tablespoon vegetable oil
- Sesame seeds, for garnish (optional)
- Sliced green onions, for garnish (optional)

Instructions:

1. Start by rehydrating the dried shredded squid. Place it in a bowl of warm water and let it soak for about 15-20 minutes until it softens. Once softened, drain the squid and squeeze out any excess water.
2. In a small bowl, mix together the soy sauce, sesame oil, and honey or sugar to create the sauce. Set it aside.
3. Heat the vegetable oil in a large skillet or wok over medium-high heat. Add the minced garlic and cook for about 30 seconds until fragrant.
4. Add the julienned carrot, thinly sliced onion, and bell peppers to the skillet. Stir-fry for about 3-4 minutes until the vegetables start to soften.
5. Add the rehydrated shredded squid to the skillet and continue to stir-fry for another 2-3 minutes until the squid is heated through.
6. Pour the sauce over the squid and vegetables in the skillet. Stir well to coat everything evenly with the sauce.
7. Continue to stir-fry for another 1-2 minutes until the sauce has thickened slightly and everything is well combined.
8. Once cooked, remove the skillet from the heat and transfer the Ojingeochae bokkeum to a serving dish.
9. Garnish with sesame seeds and sliced green onions, if desired.

10. Serve hot as a side dish with rice or as part of a Korean meal.

Enjoy the delicious flavors of Ojingeochae bokkeum! Adjust the seasoning according to your taste preferences, and feel free to add more vegetables or spice it up with some red pepper flakes if you like it spicy.

Braised dried anchovies with kelp (Myeolchi-muchim)

Ingredients:

- 1 cup dried anchovies (myeolchi), heads and guts removed
- 1 piece dried kelp (dashima or kombu), about 2x2 inches
- 2 tablespoons soy sauce
- 1 tablespoon sesame oil
- 1 tablespoon honey or sugar
- 1 clove garlic, minced
- 1 teaspoon sesame seeds
- Optional: thinly sliced green onions for garnish

Instructions:

1. Rinse the dried anchovies under cold water to remove any impurities. Drain well and pat them dry with paper towels.
2. In a small pot, combine the dried anchovies, dried kelp, soy sauce, sesame oil, honey or sugar, minced garlic, and sesame seeds.
3. Add enough water to cover the anchovies and kelp. Bring the mixture to a boil over medium-high heat.
4. Once boiling, reduce the heat to low and let it simmer for about 15-20 minutes, or until the anchovies are tender and the liquid has reduced slightly. Stir occasionally.
5. Taste the broth and adjust the seasoning if necessary, adding more soy sauce or honey/sugar according to your preference.
6. Once cooked, remove the pot from the heat and discard the dried kelp.
7. Transfer the braised anchovies to a serving dish, leaving behind any excess liquid.
8. Garnish with thinly sliced green onions, if desired.
9. Serve the Myeolchi-muchim warm or at room temperature as a side dish with rice and other Korean dishes.

Enjoy the savory and slightly sweet flavor of homemade Myeolchi-muchim! Adjust the seasoning according to your taste preferences, and feel free to add more garlic or sesame oil for extra flavor.

Stir-fried dried shredded squid with vegetables (Ojingeo chae bokkeum)

Ingredients:

- 100g dried shredded squid (ojingeo chae)
- 1 carrot, julienned
- 1 onion, thinly sliced
- 1 red bell pepper, thinly sliced
- 1 green bell pepper, thinly sliced
- 2 cloves garlic, minced
- 2 tablespoons soy sauce
- 1 tablespoon sesame oil
- 1 tablespoon honey or sugar
- 1 tablespoon vegetable oil
- Sesame seeds, for garnish (optional)
- Sliced green onions, for garnish (optional)

Instructions:

1. Start by rehydrating the dried shredded squid. Place it in a bowl of warm water and let it soak for about 15-20 minutes until it softens. Once softened, drain the squid and squeeze out any excess water.
2. Heat vegetable oil in a large skillet or wok over medium-high heat.
3. Add minced garlic to the skillet and cook for about 30 seconds until fragrant.
4. Add julienned carrots, thinly sliced onion, and bell peppers to the skillet. Stir-fry for about 3-4 minutes until the vegetables start to soften.
5. Add rehydrated shredded squid to the skillet and continue to stir-fry for another 2-3 minutes until the squid is heated through.
6. In a small bowl, mix together soy sauce, sesame oil, and honey or sugar to create the sauce.
7. Pour the sauce over the squid and vegetables in the skillet. Stir well to coat everything evenly with the sauce.
8. Continue to stir-fry for another 1-2 minutes until the sauce has thickened slightly and everything is well combined.
9. Once cooked, remove the skillet from the heat.
10. Transfer the stir-fried dried shredded squid with vegetables to a serving dish.
11. Garnish with sesame seeds and sliced green onions, if desired.

12. Serve hot as a side dish with rice or as part of a Korean meal.

Enjoy the delicious flavors of Ojingeo chae bokkeum! Adjust the seasoning according to your taste preferences, and feel free to add more vegetables or spice it up with some red pepper flakes if you like it spicy.

Spicy stir-fried squid with vegetables (Ojingeo bokkeum)

Ingredients:

- 300g squid (fresh or frozen), cleaned and cut into bite-sized pieces
- 1 onion, thinly sliced
- 1 carrot, julienned
- 1 red bell pepper, thinly sliced
- 1 green bell pepper, thinly sliced
- 3 cloves garlic, minced
- 2 tablespoons soy sauce
- 1 tablespoon gochugaru (Korean red pepper flakes)
- 1 tablespoon gochujang (Korean red pepper paste)
- 1 tablespoon sesame oil
- 1 tablespoon sugar
- 1 tablespoon vegetable oil
- Sesame seeds, for garnish (optional)
- Sliced green onions, for garnish (optional)

Instructions:

1. In a small bowl, mix together soy sauce, gochugaru, gochujang, sesame oil, and sugar to create the sauce. Set aside.
2. Heat vegetable oil in a large skillet or wok over medium-high heat.
3. Add minced garlic to the skillet and cook for about 30 seconds until fragrant.
4. Add sliced onion, julienned carrot, and thinly sliced bell peppers to the skillet. Stir-fry for about 3-4 minutes until the vegetables start to soften.
5. Add squid pieces to the skillet and continue to stir-fry for another 2-3 minutes until the squid is opaque and cooked through.
6. Pour the sauce over the squid and vegetables in the skillet. Stir well to coat everything evenly with the sauce.
7. Continue to stir-fry for another 1-2 minutes until the sauce has thickened slightly and everything is well combined.
8. Once cooked, remove the skillet from the heat.
9. Transfer the spicy stir-fried squid with vegetables to a serving dish.
10. Garnish with sesame seeds and sliced green onions, if desired.
11. Serve hot as a main dish with rice or as a side dish with other Korean dishes.

Enjoy the delicious flavors of Ojingeo bokkeum! Adjust the level of spiciness according to your taste preferences, and feel free to add more or less gochugaru or gochujang accordingly.

Stir-fried dried anchovies with peanuts (Kongari-myeolchi bokkeum)

Ingredients:

- 1 cup dried anchovies (myeolchi), heads and guts removed
- 1/2 cup peanuts
- 2 tablespoons soy sauce
- 1 tablespoon honey or sugar
- 1 tablespoon sesame oil
- 2 cloves garlic, minced
- 1 teaspoon sesame seeds
- 1 tablespoon vegetable oil

Instructions:

1. Rinse the dried anchovies under cold water to remove any impurities. Drain well and pat them dry with paper towels.
2. In a small bowl, mix together soy sauce, honey or sugar, sesame oil, minced garlic, and sesame seeds to make the sauce. Set aside.
3. Heat vegetable oil in a large skillet or non-stick pan over medium heat.
4. Add the dried anchovies to the skillet and stir-fry for 2-3 minutes, or until they are lightly browned and crispy.
5. Add the peanuts to the skillet and continue to stir-fry for another 2-3 minutes, until the peanuts are toasted and fragrant.
6. Pour the sauce over the dried anchovies and peanuts in the skillet. Stir well to coat them evenly with the sauce.
7. Continue to stir-fry for another 1-2 minutes, or until the sauce has thickened slightly and coats the anchovies and peanuts.
8. Once cooked, remove the skillet from the heat.
9. Transfer the stir-fried dried anchovies with peanuts to a serving dish.
10. Serve hot or at room temperature as a side dish or snack.

Enjoy the savory and crunchy taste of homemade Kongari-myeolchi bokkeum! Adjust the seasoning according to your taste preferences, and feel free to add more honey or sugar for your desired level of sweetness.

www.ingramcontent.com/pod-product-compliance
Lightning Source LLC
LaVergne TN
LVHW081618060526
838201LV00054B/2296